THE POWER OF INDEX FUNDS IN THE STOCK MARKET

TABLE OF CONTENTS

INTRODUCTION

To understand what an index fund is, you first need to understand what an index is. The two most commonly known indexes are the Standard & Poor (S&P) and the Dow Jones. A stock market index is a number that refers to a group of stocks. When the value of the stocks that are included in a particular index change, the index's number will change as well. If you have spent any time watching the news lately, chances are that you have heard them talk about stock indexes.

Both the S&P as well as the DOW are indexes that are made up of stocks. The DOW and the S&P are used to gauge how well the stock market is performing. An index fund is made up of a pool of money from different investors which makes it a type of mutual fund.

The main difference between a traditional mutual fund and index funds is that index funds are not actively managed while a mutual fund is. Mutual funds usually have a fund manager who focuses on buying and selling stocks to get the highest return while beating the average market percentage. An index fund, on the other hand, is managed by a computer that tracks the market and then rebalances the fund as it is needed to ensure that it matches the index that it is following.

You might be thinking that you would be better off to invest in a traditional mutual fund because you want to beat the market percentage. That is how money is made, right? Why would anyone want to invest in an index fund instead of a mutual fund?

There are a few different reasons that people choose to invest in index funds instead of a mutual fund. The first reason is that most of the time, the index fund is going to outperform mutual funds long-term. Unfortunately, the reality is most fund managers will advertise the few wins in their record only to leave out the hundreds of failures to achieve those few wins. The chances of your mutual fund manager beating the index fund over the long term is very unlikely. Fund managers that have been able to beat the market consistently over time are known as unicorns in the investment world. Unicorns because they are literally magical creatures far and few and unreachable to the common investor. In the history of investing there has been one to prove his ability to pick winning stocks again and again overtime and his name is Ray Dalio. Now to have someone like Ray Dalio manage your money you need a minimal initial investment of 100 million dollars. I tell you this to give you an idea of how rare these people are, as a matter of fact Ray Dalio no longer takes any new investors. What this means for us is that the fund managers available to us simply don't have the knowledge and ability to make their promises come true. Therefore, placing your investments in the stock market in three strategic index funds you can have an investment plan that promises not to be diluted by fund manager fees and greed. It is common practice for fund managers to come up with new fees finding new ways to siphon money from your investment gains.

The second reason is that most people who invest in the market do not have a lot of knowledge about the market. An index fund allows a person who does not have a lot of investing knowledge to succeed in the market. The final reason is that it is more likely that you will keep your returns when you invest in an index fund rather than if you invested in a traditional mutual fund. Given the total amount of fees and commissions paid in mutual funds.

CHAPTER 1: ESSENTIAL TOOL FOR THE COMMON INVESTOR

While there are a lot of great advantages to index funds, especially for investors who are just starting or those who do not have a lot of money to invest in the market, there are a few things that you need to know. First, index funds are not magical. There are good investments, bad investments, and mediocre investments. Simply investing in an index fund does not mean that you are going to see returns on your investment. You do have to ensure that you are investing in a reliable index fund that has a good history of providing returns. When choosing an index fund you can research price history. I like to look at the last 10 years or more of the index funds price history. You will notice the increase in price over time and also notice the drops in price that occur over time. It's important to understand this, in a later chapter we will talk about how emotions play a big part of investing. Your emotions can definitely get in the way of making rational decisions especially with the type of value and meaning that we put behind our money.

Things like a correction happen on average once a year. A correction is a drop in price of stocks in the market, usually 10%, now when the correction occurs and you panic and sell your index funds only to see the price come back up within a few months you have now experienced an irrational decision in investing affected by your emotions. Experts recommend you invest into your index funds monthly, set it and forget it. Spending too much time listening to the news and checking your Investments every day can only cause you to doubt your strategy when the inevitable drops in price occur.

Another common part of investing is a market crash, one that happens on average every 3 to 5 years usually resulting in a 20% drop in price. This is another scenario that causes investors to sell from the fear of losing more of their money. Experts like Warren Buffett time and time again tell us that when there's a market crash that's an opportunity to buy stocks on sale. In 2008 when the big housing market crash occurred and investors lost billions overnight, Many people sold their stocks for very low prices and smart investors bought only to see the biggest bounce back of the market, resulting in a rise in the market of 200% over the next 5 years. Those who stayed the course and continued to invest even through the tough times reaped the benefits of the U.S. markets ability to grow and bounce back over the long term.

A great advantage of investing into your index funds monthly is a little something called dollar cost averaging. This concept is based on your ability to capture your index funds at different prices throughout your investment career. Meaning that because of the market volatility there will be times when you capture your index funds at lower prices increasing your total gains when the market recovers from those temporary drops in price. A common scenario for an untrained investor is to buy when there's a lot of hype around a stock, a stock which has been rising in price hence the hype. So he now purchases that stock which usually by the time he's heard about it is reaching its peak price then suddenly it begins to drop, then continues to drop he now sells the stock for fear of losing all his money. This is a perfect example of buying high selling low, which is disastrous in investing. Yet this practice is very common. The reality is that you do not lock in a loss until you sell your stock or Index Fund. This means that when you buy and hold your index funds long term you will experience market corrections and crashes, but as lons as you don't sell you haven't experienced any loss. The value will bounce back and continue its average growth of 7% – 10% per year over 10+ year periods.

The index fund is going to allow a person to invest small amounts of money into the market while lowering the cost of their transactions. What this means is that if you are investing 10,000 dollars into the market, if you are using a brokerage account, most of your principle is going to be eaten up by commissions. This is especially true if you are trying to build your portfolio as you try to buy 30, 40, or more stocks through a brokerage account. Your broker will charge you to buy the stocks, charge you to move your money from one stock to another in order to "optimize your gains", which as we explained doesn't result in any added gains at all just another fee, and you will also pay taxes on that money he is actively moving around. As you may see fees, commissions, and taxes can easily eat up most of your gains.

Index funds are not actively managed therefore they produce minimal fees to the investor. Once you have held your investments for 1 year or more you will only pay a tax called capital gains tax. This tax is much smaller than that paid of an investment sold within a year of its purchase. The average turnover of actively managed funds on a yearly basis is 89%. This means that of all the money invested in mutual funds 89% of that money is moved from one stock to another every year resulting in millions of dollars in fees paid by you the investor. A great strategy to slowly syphon money from you and into the pockets of wall street.

One of the best things about investing in an index fund is that they are low-turnover. What this means is that most investors will make their investment and then stick with it. They are ghost ship portfolios. It does take a lot of mental effort to not sell when the market drops. However, when a person invests this way, they can see huge rewards over the long-term. You don't have to worry about the everyday ups and downs of the market.

It has been shown that when a person invests in index funds and continues to invest even when the market is down, they will see huge returns over a long period. We are talking about long-term investments of 10 to 50 years.

Index funds are, by nature, diversified. This means that by investing in index funds, your portfolio is already diversified. Why is diversification important? Diversification is going to reduce your risks when you are investing in the market.

Investing in an index fund is also going to ensure that you are not investing in companies that you do not understand. Many people invest in the stock market but do not understand the companies that they are investing in. They will throw their entire life savings into a company that they think is going to do well even when there is no reason for them to believe it to be so. By investing in an index fund, they are putting their money in the hands of people who have more experience in investing and are working to make the best decisions when it comes to the money that they are investing.

The index fund is very important for the common investor, a person who does not have all day long to spend watching the stock market and doing research on the different stocks. Index funds are the best bet for those that have a modest portfolio and don't know what they are doing when it comes to investing in the stock market. Your index fund will be invested in the best companies across many industries and many markets. A total U.S. market fund, bought through a company like Vanguard, has approximately 3,600 stocks all in one index fund. As you may see it's very diversified.

This strategy is going to ensure that you do not have to spend hour upon hour pouring over information about each company that you are considering investing in, while never knowing if you are making the best decision.

An index fund is a great tool that has the potential to save you a lot of money while helping you build a nice portfolio. Once you have increased your wealth enough by using index funds you can gamble a bit and invest into specific stocks you may like.

Index funds are a tool that should be used when it is in your best interest. There is no reason for anyone to avoid them, but instead, they should be used to grow wealth.

CHAPTER 2: ADVANTAGES OF DIVERSIFICATION IN INDEX FUNDS

Every investment comes with the opportunity to see returns, but it also comes with some risks. A few of the different risks include:

- Losing money
- Due to price volatility, your money may not be available when you need it, or you may risk losing money to access it when it is needed.
- Emotional stress due to the volatility of the market. A person may struggle emotionally when they fear losing money on the market. This can lead to buying or selling at the wrong time.

Whenever a stock, or a group of stocks, is subject to the same possible effects, you need to diversify away from that specific group of stocks to minimize your risks.

What is diversification? Diversification can be described as a risk management technique by investing in a variety of different investments within your portfolio. The reason for diversification is that when a portfolio contains different types of assets, it will usually yield higher returns while reducing any risks for the individual.

Diversification is one of the most important tools that a person can use when it comes to investing. It is a critical aspect of investing in the stock market. The good news for investors is that by investing in index funds, the job of diversification is made much easier than if they were investing individual stocks or bonds. The index funds holdings are already diversified.

Simply put, diversification means that you do not put all your eggs in one basket. It means that you are spreading your investments across different types of assets. Index funds make this very easy to do.

Diversification is one of the many different advantages when it comes to investing in index funds. Index funds allow for instant diversification as well as portfolio diversification in multiple categories. The great thing about index funds is that you can invest a couple of thousand dollars in one index fund and instantly obtain a diversified portfolio. If you were to try to diversify your portfolio on your own, you would need to purchase a lot of individual securities, which would expose you to more risk than an index fund would.

The index fund is also going to allow diversification between sectors, styles, and any combination of securities that can be imagined.

While index funds are an amazing tool when it comes to diversification, many people tend to make a very common mistake. They tend to believe that because they are putting their money into different stocks, their portfolio is diversified. Different does not mean diverse. For example, if you are purchasing stocks for different companies but they are all part of the same sector, your portfolio will not be diversified. An index fund takes the chances of you making this mistake away.

To truly diversify your portfolio, you will need to invest in investment funds that do not have shareholdings with your other investments. Make sure that you are considering the holdings within your index fund that you are investing in as you spread your investments throughout different types of index funds.

In summary, investing in index funds is going to allow for diversification between different stocks while also allowing you to invest in different sectors. By using diversification, you can reduce your risks in one specific stock or sector. This opens the potential for you to see more returns in your investments.

In other words, diversification is going to allow you to grow your wealth over time while minimizing your risks, which is what investing in the stock market is all about.

CHAPTER 3:
INVESTING MADE EASY

When it comes to investing, most people think that it is too complicated for them to understand. However, just like everything else in life, investing can be learned. If you are one of those people that have always felt that investing is too complicated, I have good news for you. Investing in the market does not have to be complicated at all. This is especially true when you choose to invest in index funds.

If you want to grow your wealth, you are going to need to do more than just put your money in a savings account. This is especially true today given what the interest rate is compared to the inflation rate. Investing in the market is one of the ways that you can use to grow your wealth.

One of the greatest benefits of an index fund is that they are not managed by a fund manager, which allows you to avoid high fees. Most index funds are going to cost very little, usually ½ of a percent of the assets. This means that you are going to be able to keep more of your returns, which will allow you to grow your wealth even more. When you choose to invest in index funds, you are not spending your time trying to outperform the market. Many fund managers make the promise that they will outperform the market, but this does not happen most of the time. While it may be their goal, it does not always happen.

Choosing to invest in index funds means that you know exactly what you are getting. All you must do is track the index. What this means is that if the index increases 5% you will know that your money will increase 5% as well. The same goes for a decline. If the index decreases by 2%, you know that your money will decline by 2%.

Why would this be a benefit to index funds? According to studies done by S&P, most managers underperform the market average. What this tells us is that while a manager may promise to outperform the stock market, the chances are that they will underperform. Most people who invest in the market would rather know exactly what they are getting instead of putting their money in the hands of someone who is not going to be able to keep their promises.

What types of index funds can an investor invest in? The great thing about investing in index funds is that by investing in 3 index funds, you can cover all your bases. These include:

- The US bond market
- The US stock market
- The International market

How much should you invest into stocks and how much in bonds. a commonly used formula Is to have your age and bonds. If you're 40 years old you'd have 40% in bonds and 60% in stocks. If you're 30 you have 30% in bonds 70% in stocks. Someone who is 30 may decide to go 20% in bonds 80% in stocks. Stocks have a higher potential return than bonds. Someone who has time to bounce back from a market crash may decide to invest more in stocks while someone who's getting close to retirement may decide to have more money in bonds, given they are less volatile and more secure for when the money is needed. By first understanding this structure you then can begin to tailor your investment strategy according to your own risk threshold.

When choosing stocks you will see three options, amongst others, known as large-cap, mid-cap and small-cap. What this means is the size and revenue of the companies involved in these index funds. Mid-cap and small-cap have higher return potentials but also higher risk involved. While a good portion of your investment in stocks should be on large cap feel free to use part of your stock investment in some of the medium and small cap options. This is your chance to risk a little with the confidence that your main strategy will allow your money to grow over time creating a nice nest egg for your retirement.

How can you invest in these index funds? The first thing that you will want to do is to choose a firm that is a leader in index fund investing. These include companies such as Vanguard as well as TD Ameritrade, and Fidelity. These three specific companies charge extremely low fees and provide great customer service. However, you should do your own research when it comes to the company that you want to use. I personally utilize Vanguard. Vanguard has been a pioneer in the world of index funds. They have helped level the playing field for the common investor.

When creating an account, you will have three options. Lets begin with the IRA (individual retirement account). There are 2 options within this category Roth and traditional IRA. The major difference lies within its method of being taxed. A traditional IRA is tax deferred, which means you don't pay taxes on that money invested until you sell your investments. If you make $50,000 in one year and invest $4,000 in your traditional IRA, that year when you do your taxes you only pay taxes for $46,000 of earned income. Many people like this idea of paying taxes later. The problem with this, is over time history has shown us one thing and that's taxes are always rising and never falling. Therefore, if you choose to pay taxes on this money 10-30 years later when you decide to retire, your tax bracket may be higher than it's now. Resulting in higher taxes paid.

Now lets see our other choice within IRA. The Roth IRA, which is the opposite. You pay taxes on the money now as you usually do and whatever that money produces in gains from now on is tax-free and can be withdrawn early without penalty fees. Withdrawing early isn't recommended as it reduces how much of your money is compounding and growing but I understand emergencies happen.

The third choice is a brokerage account which you manage. Yet, unlike mutual funds you will not be actively moving the money around resulting in taxes and fees. You will purchase and hold for the long-term.

Any of the three choices you make will only consume about 15 to 20 minutes of your time every month. Time in which you will spend transferring funds from you banking account into your investment account. Then buying index funds based on your current portfolio percentages. More on that shortly.

If you already have an account with a stockbroker, it is very easy to buy index funds. Just let your broker know that is what you want to do, and they will do it for you. It is important to know that you may get some resistance from your broker because they know that when you switch to indexing, they will not be trading, and trading creates a bigger commission for them.

If you choose to go with an index investor, you will find that it only takes about 30 minutes to open a new index fund account. You will want to start with investing in domestic index funds, like the S&P. Next, you will have to decide whether you want to invest in an international index fund. It is important to know that many companies such as Coca Cola, while they are domestic companies, earn most of their profits internationally. On the other hand, there are international companies, such as BP, that will earn most of their profits in the states.

If you choose to maximize your diversification, you will go in both markets. Because the markets are going to fluctuate differently, after the first year, you may want to rebalance your investments back to your original structure. If you choose to use an index fund investing company, you don't have to worry about rebalancing, it is taken care of for you.

You may prefer less international diversification. If that is the case, just choose whatever you are comfortable with. This could be 10%, 20%, or 30%.

Are you enjoying this book so far? An Amazon review means so much to authors, we use them to grow and they also help others reach this content.

CHAPTER 4: TWO BIGGEST ENEMIES OF INVESTING; EMOTIONS AND FEES

Emotions play a part in our everyday lives. However, they should never play a part in investing. The worst investment decisions are made when the investor allows their emotions to take over. Never allow yourself to become emotionally attached to any of your investments. When you are investing, you need to make sure that you can think rationally. You also need to make sure that you can stay calm and do not allow your emotions to take over. There are three different emotions that you need to be very careful of when you are investing in the market.

Fear

Back in March of 2009, the market lows provided investors with amazing opportunities to purchase stocks for pennies on the dollar. Companies such as GE, Wells Fargo, and Bank of America were trading extremely low. Why did more investors not grab up shares of these companies? Because of fear. Fear is one of the biggest enemies of investing because it is going to stop you from taking advantage of opportunities that happen once in a lifetime. The best time for a person to invest in the stock market is when the general public is experiencing fear.

Anger

Sometimes investors will sell a great investment because they are frustrated by the performance, only to see that the stock surges after it is sold. There are far too many occasions when an investor sells an investment out of frustration only to see it perform well after they sell it. Anger can make you reject an amazing idea simply because you are tired of the slow progress.

When you overreact with anger, you will only rob yourself of some of your best investments and ideas. If you give in to the anger, you will end up even more frustrated than you were before. Remember, when it comes to investing you must always remain calm, even when you don't like what is happening. Stay focused on your reason for investing, and do not let your emotions get in your way.

Greed

Whenever you make an investment you need to make sure that you know the exit point in advance. By choosing what your exit point is going to be, you will be able to ensure that emotions such as greed to not affect your investments. No matter what your investment is, stocks, bonds, real estate, and so on, you must know at what price you are going to sell. So many investors hold on to their investments out of their greed.

Greed can cause an investor to hold on to a high valued stock, until it drops in value, in the hope that it will continue to raise. Greed can cause real estate investors to continue to buy property even when they know that the prices are far too high. Don't get too attached to any specific investment. Remind yourself that you are not going to hold on to the stock forever, and the purpose is to make a profit.

Enemy #2- Fees

Emotions are not the only enemy of investing. Fees are another enemy that you need to be aware of. No matter what type of investing that you take part in, they all come with a cost. I am not just talking about opportunity costs when you choose to invest in one asset instead of a different one. But instead, I am talking about costs that many investors completely forget about or just choose to ignore. Investors may choose to ignore these costs because they are confusing and may be found in the fine print. However, all investors need to understand the different types of costs.

Different types of investments are going to carry different costs. For example, mutual funds, no matter what type, charge an expense ratio. The expense ratio is the cost of managing the fund, and it is expressed as a percentage. This percentage is based on the total amount invested and it is calculated each year. This fee is usually paid out of the fund. This means that it is not something that you are billed for, but instead, it will come out of your returns.

In other words, if your returns are 8% and your expense ratio of 1.5% is taken out of your returns, you will only see a return of 6.5% on your investments.

There are a couple of different problems with this. First is that a high amount of your money is going to your management team instead of going into your pocket. Secondly, the more the management team charges, the harder it becomes for the mutual fund to match the market's performance. Many of these mutual funds will claim that the extra cost is worth the returns that you will see. However, the expense ratios slowly drain your returns. In other words, the higher the fees, the lower the chances of you earning a return on your investments. Therefore, many people choose to invest in index funds. There is no management team.

Some companies are going to charge marketing costs. What are these? Simply put it is a fee that you are going to pay for the managers to promote a mutual fund to those that may potentially invest. This is called a 12B-1 Fee.

Annual and custodian fees are another type of fee that you need to be careful of when you are investing. These usually apply to IRAs or other retirement accounts. They are usually between 25 and 90 dollars each year. These fees are used to cover the costs that come with IRS reporting regulations.

You may also come across purchase or redemption fees, which will be a specific percentage of the value of the stock that you are buying or selling. There is also a front-end load fee that is charged when you buy shares as well as a back-end load fee, which is charged when you sell shares. Then some commissions are going to be paid to the broker.

At this point, you can probably tell that brokers have not made investing in the market easy. When you consider all these fees you may be wondering how a person can see any returns on their investments. That is exactly why fees are the enemy of investing, they will eat up every penny of your returns.

The problem with fees is that they almost always appear low. The investor may see an expense ratio of 1.5% and completely dismiss it as insignificant. The problem is that it's not. When a fee is expressed in a percentage it doesn't express to investors how much money they will be charged or how much of their returns it will eat up.

Let's look at an example:

If you invest $80,000 and you hold on to your investments for 25 years, during those 25 years, you are averaging 7% each year while paying out .5% in fees annually. At the end of that 25 years, you will have made about $380,000. However, if you are being charged 2% in fees each year, you are only going to have $260,000. That is $120,000 extra that will be paid out in fees.

Most people would look at that 2% fee as a tiny fee. However, when you look at how much it can cost you over the long term, you can tell how these fees are the enemy of investing.

The good news is that time and again studies have proven that the lower-cost funds will provide better returns than the higher-cost funds. Even the cheapest funds have been proven to outperform the most expensive ones when it comes to long-term investing.

CHAPTER 5: SIMPLE LONG-TERM INVESTING STRATEGY THAT YOU CAN USE

There are hundreds of different people out there telling investors how they can make money on the market. While their techniques may work, it is important to keep things simple while ensuring that you are going to increase your returns and reduce your risks.

Investing in low-cost index funds is going to help you to increase your wealth while providing you with a diversified portfolio. It is also going to ensure that you are not spending all your time focusing on the market. Index funds are great investments for those that want to continue working their regular job and not spend all their time following the market.

When you invest in an index fund, the investment should be long term - meaning between 10-30 years or longer. The first thing that you are going to want to do is to decide what you want to invest in. S&P, for example, contains the largest companies that make up the stock market. You can invest in the DOW or any other index fund that you are interested in.

You will want to take some time to think about the index fund that you want to invest in. What do you want your risk level to be? What other assets are you invested in? Stocks are usually seen as a riskier investment than bonds because the price of stocks will fluctuate more. However, stocks are going to provide you with the potential for larger returns.

The next thing that you want to do is to check what the minimum investment amount is. Most index funds are going to have a minimum investment, which can range from 1 to 3,000 dollars. If you do not have enough money to invest in a particular index fund, you can mark that index fund off of your potential investments for right now.

Make sure that you look for index funds that have an expense ratio of around .5%. It does not matter if you are investing in an IRA, a 401K, or another index fund, you want to make sure that the expense ratio is less than 1%, ideally, the expense ratio should be about .5% or even lower. If your expense ratio is .5% you will be paying $5 for every $1000 of your balance each year.

Because index funds do not require much attention, they tend to cost much less. Those that use a Robo-advisor will pay even less than those that use a manager.

You will then want to fund your investment. Make sure that you fund this investment with money that you can afford to lose. Never take out a loan to fund your investment, never borrow money from your friends and family to fund your investment, and do not fund your investments with your credit card.

You will also want to set up automatic contributions. How much do you want to invest each week or each month? If you are investing in your 401k that will be automatically taken out of your salary each time you get paid, but if you are investing in a different index fund you will need to set up the contributions. Make sure that you are only investing what you can afford.

When you are investing in the stock market, you must ignore all the fluctuations that you see and stay the course. Remember that no matter how many times the market drops, it always goes back up again.

What About Compound Interest?

Over time, a person can build a nice nest egg by using compound interest. The best investments are going to provide you with compound returns. This means that no matter what is going on in the stock market, you will have the magic of compounding on your side.

Simple interest is what a financial institution is going to pay you based on the amount of money that you put into your savings account. For example, if you put $1,000 into your savings account, and you have a 2.5 APR, you will receive $25 in interest in a year. You will continue to receive $25 in interest every year that you leave your $1,000 in the savings account.

Now let's take that same $1,000 and look at how it would work if it received the same 2.5% interest rate but compounded. In the first year, you are going to get $25 in interest. In the second year, you are going to receive that original $25 as well as interest on the $25 that you earned the previous year. By the third year, you will receive the $25 as well as interest off all the interest that was paid to you the previous two years.

What is going to affect what you earn? The initial investment is going to affect what you earn. Imagine that instead of putting $1,000 into the account you put in $10,000 even at a 2.5% interest rate, you are going to see some substantial growth fairly quickly.

The next thing that you will want to think about is how much you can contribute each month. While you do not have to continue to add to the account each month it is highly recommended. You should also think about how long you plan on leaving this money in the savings account. Of course, the longer you leave the money in the account, the more interest you are going to earn.

What is the interest rate? Your interest rate is going to affect how much money you earn from your savings. You should also look at how often your interest is going to compound. For example, the interest could compound yearly, every six months, once a month, or even daily. The more often that the interest compounds, the more money you stand to make.

How can you take advantage of compound interest? You will want to look for a high yield savings account. Find a lender with the highest interest rate. This means that you will receive the highest return. Some lenders are going to require a minimum investment and you will want to make sure that you have this amount of money before you sign up.

Once you have received interest payments, take that money and put it back into the investment account. The more money that you put into the account, the higher your rate of return will be. You will also want to make sure that you are looking for a bank or a broker that is going to charge low monthly fees for maintaining your account. You do not want to lose all your returns to fees.

Taking advantage of compound interest is a great way for people who do not want to take any risk on the stock market to grow their wealth. Place your emergency fund or other money that you do not want to risk on the market into an account that will provide you with compound interest so that you can see the biggest returns without risking a single penny of your money.

CHAPTER 6: 401K, IRA- ROTH AND TRADITIONAL, PERSONAL BROKERAGE ACCOUNT

I'm interested in beginning my investment career, where do I start? You have three good options; IRA traditional, Roth, and personal brokerage account. Lets break them down and see how to make best use of them. We will consider the taxes, fees, and limitations that come with each option. Lets also dive into what this means for those with a 401k.

IRA (Individual Retirement Account) – TRADITIONAL

The biggest appeal of the traditional IRA is that it is a tax deferred investment. What this means is that it will be a deduction on your taxes. If you made $60,000 in 2019 and invested $5,000 into your Traditional IRA than you will pay taxes on $55,000 that year.

How about withdrawing the money? Well, all withdraws are subject to ordinary income tax. Any withdrawal done before the age of 59 1/2 will result in an additional 10% federal penalty tax.

What this means for us as investors is that we must make sure to have an emergency fund in our savings account. Money that is readily available in case your car breaks down or any other emergency. Many financial advisors will suggest $2,000 is a good place to start. This will keep you from having to sell any of your investments because you need the cash. Your strategy is to invest for the long term, therefore the goal is to not touch the money and allow it to grow.

Your traditional IRA does have a yearly contribution limit. The limits are $6,000 per year for those age 50 and under and $7,000 per year for those age 5o or older. Finally, this option has a RMU (required minimum distribution) once you hit the age of 70 ½. This means you will have to withdraw a certain amount of your investments annually and no longer be able to invest into traditional IRA.

IRA (Individual Retirement Account) – Roth

The Roth IRA has a different set of appeals like no withdrawal fees, no required minimum distribution, no age limits to contribute. Given you will not be able to deduct this contribution from your taxes you will have already paid income taxes on this money, allowing it to grow tax-free. Any quantity you contribute can be withdrawn. If you withdraw from any of the money's growth before age 59 1/2 , than you can expect some fees and penalties. After age 59 ½ you can withdraw from your earnings without any fees. The Roth IRA has the same contribution limits as the traditional.

Lets analyze the tax situation for both your Roth and Traditional. Its important to understand that history has shown us that tax rates always rise over the years. Our Leaders continue to raise the debt of our country and it becomes more and more evident that most of the time the solution is to throw money at problems and hopefully they fix themselves. Unfortunately, the real outcome is that the debt is inherited by us the taxpayers. The taxes will continue to rise to maintain the overspending that occurs from government year after year. What does this mean for your investment career? Well, I believe that a Roth IRA will make more sense, given you pay taxes now at the current tax rate. As appose to deferring your tax payment to 10-30 years from now when taxes are most likely higher for you.

Individual Brokerage Account

This account is a good option if you're maxing out your yearly contributions to Roth and or Traditional IRA's. This account type allows withdrawals before retirement age like a Roth. A brokerage account can be a great way to save for a house, college fund, retirement.

401K

What is my advice on 401K? Well, the truth is I'm not very convinced by the many companies that provide 401k services. The simple reason is fees and commissions. Once again, we go back to the concept of optimizing your gains by reducing your overall cost of investment. By learning to invest on your own with the strategies we have spoken about you will eliminate the management cost of the company's managing your 401k. Therefore, leaving more of the gains in your pocket and not in the pockets of managers. Now, if your employer matches you any percentage of contribution, then by all means take advantage of that money. Not taking advantage of whatever, your employer will match is leaving free money on the table.

Conclusion

Investing in the stock market can seem confusing when you are first starting. If you have tried to learn about investing only to find yourself more confused than you were before, don't feel bad.

There is so much complex information out there about investing in the stock market that it can make investing seem unattainable.

While many people want to overcomplicate investing in the stock market, I have good news for you. None of it is necessary. By investing in index funds and allowing your investment to grow over a long period, you will be able to grow your wealth while avoiding all the overcomplicated information out there.

Index funds are a great investment for people who just don't have the time to go out and learn everything there is to know about the stock market. You can think of an index fund as a set it and forget it system. When you invest in an index fund, you don't let the inevitable fluctuations of the market pull you from your course. Instead, you leave your investment, continue to add to it, and allow it to grow as the market begins to rise again.

By doing this you will take all the emotions out of investing, and you will be setting yourself up with a nice little nest egg for the future.

Please subscribe with your email to my website at https://www.tapyourpower.org/. Upon subscribing you will receive a FREE Copy of my new e-book on Leadership titled, "**5 Essential Leadership Qualities**"

And finally, if you liked the book, I would like to ask you to do me a favor and leave a review for the book on Amazon. Reviews help us the authors grow and learn how to add more value with your feedback. They also help us get the content to many more readers.

Thank you and Good Luck!!